I AM A JAGUAR

Steve Macleod

MEDIA ENHANCED BOOKS
AV² BY WEIGL™
ADDED VALUE • AUDIO VISUAL

Go to **www.av2books.com**, and enter this book's unique code.

BOOK CODE

D 548334

AV² by Weigl brings you media enhanced books that support active learning.

AV² provides enriched content that supplements and complements this book. Weigl's AV² books strive to create inspired learning and engage young minds in a total learning experience.

Your AV² Media Enhanced books come alive with...

Audio
Listen to sections of the book read aloud.

Video
Watch informative video clips.

Embedded Weblinks
Gain additional information for research.

Try This!
Complete activities and hands-on experiments.

Key Words
Study vocabulary, and complete a matching word activity.

Quizzes
Test your knowledge.

Slide Show
View images and captions, and prepare a presentation.

... and much, much more!

Published by AV² by Weigl
350 5th Avenue, 59th Floor New York, NY 10118
Website: www.av2books.com www.weigl.com

Macleod, Steve.
Jaguar / Steve Macleod.
     p. cm. -- (I am)
  ISBN 978-1-61690-758-7 (hardcover : alk. paper) -- ISBN 978-1-61690-851-5 (softcover : alk. paper)
1. Jaguar--Juvenile literature. I. Title.
  QL737.C23M184 2011
  599.75'5--dc22

                              2010052410

Printed in the United States of America in North Mankato, Minnesota
1 2 3 4 5 6 7 8 9 0 15 14 13 12 11

052011
WEP37500

Project Coordinator: Aaron Carr   Art Director: Terry Paulhus

Weigl acknowledges Getty Images as the primary image supplier for this title.

I AM A JAGUAR

In this book, I will teach you about

- myself

- my food

- my home

- my family

and much more!

3

I am a jaguar.

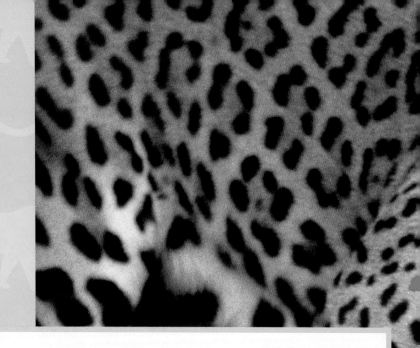

I use my spots
to hide from other animals.

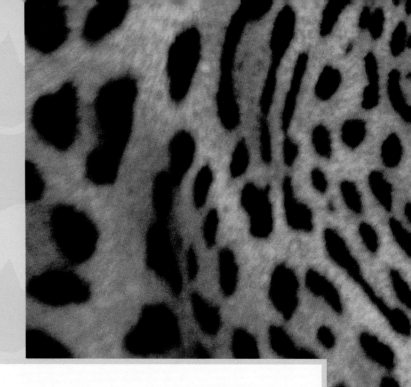

I feel with my whiskers.

8

I look for food at night.

10

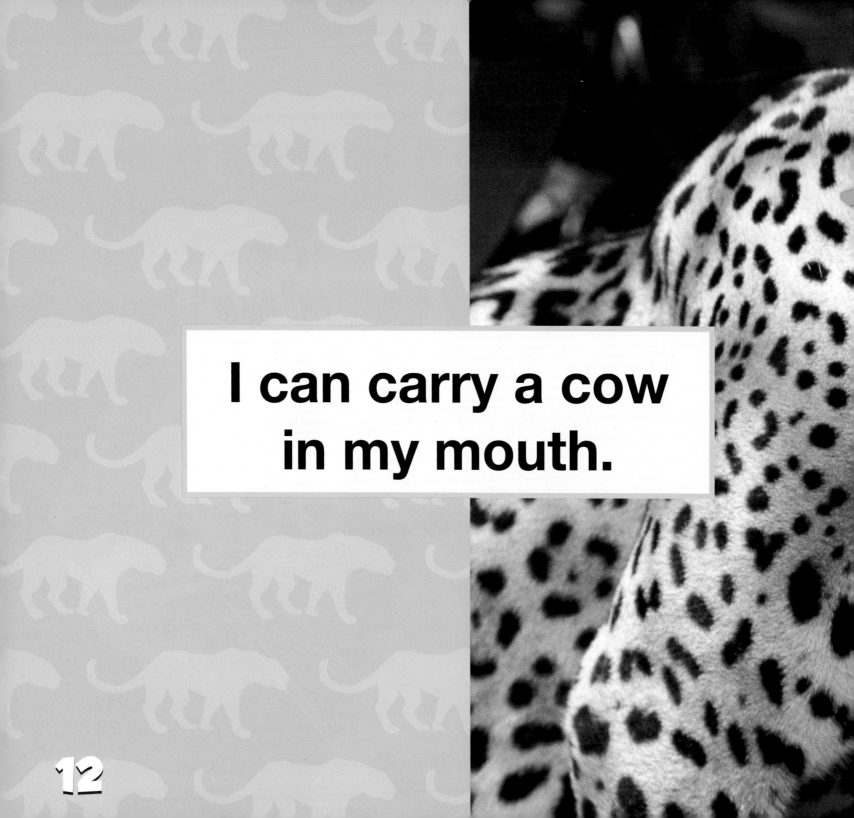

I can carry a cow
in my mouth.

13

I scratch trees to tell other cats where I live.

I can not see
for two weeks
after I am born.

I swim
with my head
above water.

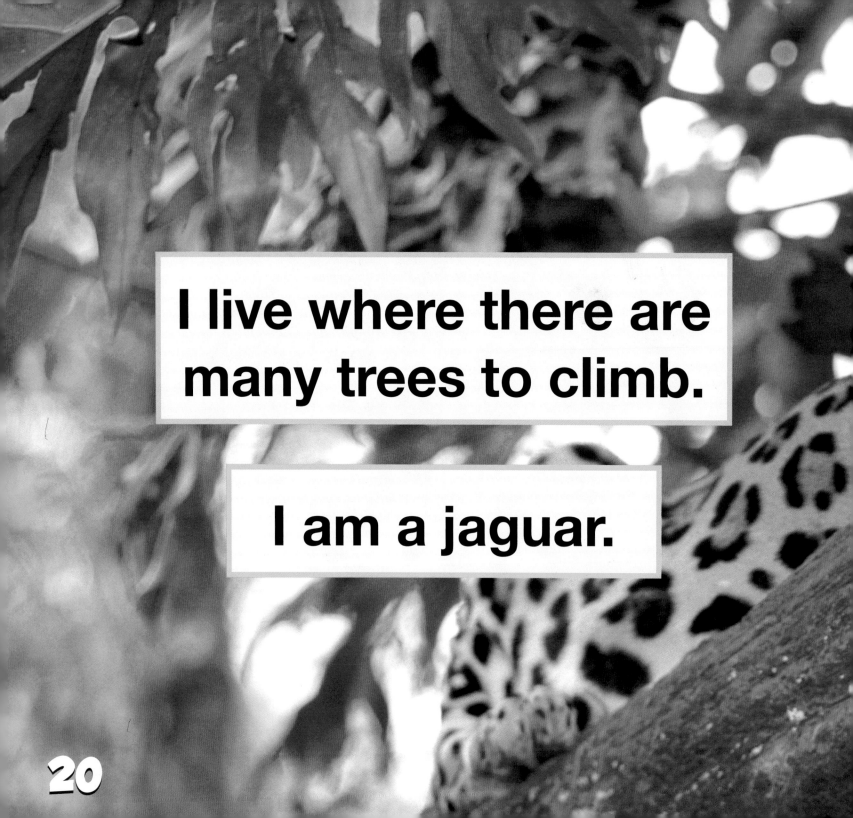

I live where there are many trees to climb.

I am a jaguar.

20

JAGUAR FACTS

This page provides more detail about the interesting facts found in the book. Simply look for the corresponding page number to match the fact.

Pages 4-5

I am a jaguar. Jaguars are the largest spotted cat in the world. Like most cats, jaguars have round heads, whiskers, large eyes, curved and sharp claws, and strong and compact bodies. The heaviest jaguar ever recorded weighed 348 pounds (158 kilograms). That is more than the weight of 38 house cats.

Pages 6–7

Jaguars use their spots to hide from other animals. The spots on a jaguar's fur are called rosettes. The rosettes help jaguars hide in tall grass and trees. Blending in with their surroundings helps jaguars sneak up on other animals when they are hunting.

Pages 8–9

Jaguars feel with their whiskers. This is how jaguars can feel what is around them. It is the same as how people can feel what is around them using their fingers. Jaguars also use their sense of smell and hearing to hunt for food.

Pages 10–11

Jaguars look for food at night. They can see very well in the dark. Hunting at night helps jaguars sneak up on their prey, so they do not have to chase the animal. Jaguars have powerful jaws and sharp teeth, which also help them hunt.

Pages 12–13

Jaguars can carry a cow in their mouth. They have been seen dragging animals that weigh 800 pounds (364 kg). That is more than four times the weight of an average jaguar. Jaguars eat many different animals, including mammals, reptiles, birds, and fish.

Pages 14–15

Jaguars scratch trees to make notes for other cats. Jaguars prefer to live and hunt by themselves. They scratch trees to mark their territory. This lets other jaguars know that they live there.

Pages 16–17

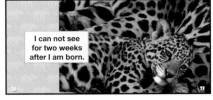

Jaguars can not see for two weeks after they are born. They keep their eyes shut for up to 13 days after they are born. Baby jaguars are called cubs. The cubs weigh less than 2 pounds (0.9 kg) when they are born.

Pages 18–19

Jaguars swim with their head above water. Unlike many other cats, jaguars do not avoid water. They spend much of their time near water, and they can swim across wide rivers. Jaguars also go into the water to cool down.

Pages 20–21

Jaguars live where there are many trees to climb. Most jaguars live in the rainforests of South America. Some of these forests are being cut down to make more room for humans to live. Jaguars are a threatened species. There are only about 15,000 jaguars left in the world.

WORD LIST

Research has shown that as much as 65 percent of all written material published in English is made up of 300 words. These 300 words cannot be taught using pictures or learned by sounding them out. They must be recognized by sight. This book contains 30 common sight words to help young readers improve their reading fluency and comprehension. This book also teaches young readers several important content words, such as proper nouns. These words are paired with pictures to aid in learning and improve understanding.

Page	Sight Words
4	a, am, I
6	from, I, my, other, to, use
8	I, my, with
10	at, food, for, I, look, night
12	a, can, carry, I, in, my
14	I, live, other, tell, to, tree, where
16	after, am, can, for, I, not, see, two
18	head, I, my, water, with
20	a, am, are, I, live, many, there, to, tree, where

Page	Content Words
4	jaguar
6	animal, hide, spot
8	feel, whisker
10	
12	cow, mouth
14	cat, scratch
16	born, week
18	above, swim
20	climb, jaguar